Beneath Western Skies

a SiarScéal anthology

First Published in 2020 by The Manuscript Publisher
ISBN: 978-1-911442-28-8
A CIP Catalogue record for this book is available from the
National Library

Typesetting, page design and layout, cover design by
DocumentsandManuscripts.com
Cover photographs by Anni Wilton-Jones

Published, printed and bound in Ireland

Beneath Western Skies

RCN: 20201056
www.SiarSceal.com

Foreword

Beneath Western Skies anthology is comprised from Roscommon County Libraries regional programme of external library literary events and the SiarScéal collaborative fits this remit. Since 2007, SiarScéal Festival has been hosted in their premises.

It is from the essence of oneself that creative writing is expressed and throughout this anthology, from adults to children, the raw rugged countryside, rivers, lakes and waves in splendour unfold as you flick from page to page.

SiarScéal Festival celebrates the regional environs through literature and all art forms, particularly poetry, to art, photography and choral recitals. The Hanna Greally International Literary Award-winning writers and students are the creative force, participating also in the *Beneath Western Skies* ongoing exhibition, launched in Roscommon Library and on tour with Ballinamore and Tubbercurry Libraries.

Anni Wilton-Jones' children's collective of West of Ireland poetry to photography was the inspirational muse for the children's workshops. Anni is published in a number of journals including *Cúirt Journal*, *Of Sawn Grain* and *Salvo* and her repertoire also includes *Fresh Voices for Younger Listeners* and other collections and CDs. *Beneath Western Skies* anthology is compiled and edited by her.

Gwen McNamara Bond
SiarScéal Festival Founder/Director

Preface

SiarScéal Festival is an annual event that celebrates the history, culture and literary life of County Roscommon, whilst welcoming the involvement of writers from across Ireland and beyond. The festival is generously hosted by Roscommon County Council Library Services and is supported by both the Library Service and other benefactors, as shown on the acknowledgements page elsewhere in this book.

The festival is built around the Hanna Greally International Literary Awards. As well as offering writing awards for both children and adults, the festival provides workshops for children and events for people of all ages.

This anthology reflects the work of the festival and its attendees over the last three years. It is directed at poetry, rather than prose and includes poems and illustrations.

The opening section, *Reflections on Climate Change*, consists of specially commissioned poems by adults, young people and children. Some of these poems came from workshops for children, run by Gwen McNamara Bond. Two of the poems were written especially for the anthology by guest writer, Faye Boland.

The second and third sections contain a selection of poems from:

- Hanna Greally Awards for adults (2019) – theme of *Western Medley Recital*
- Hanna Greally Awards for children (2019)
- *Beneath Western Skies* exhibition on tour (2019) – poems by children, along with the trigger materials created for the children's workshops.
- *Beneath Western Skies* exhibition (2018) – work from

writers of all ages, illustrated by photographs and drawings

How does one go about choosing works to be included in an anthology, knowing that some writers will, unfortunately, have to be disappointed? In my case, I decided that it was important to demonstrate the wide range of interpretations of the *Western* themes and the variety of styles chosen. I therefore decided to limit every writer represented in the second and third sections to a single item, so as to include as many poets as possible.

I certainly considered the judgement of others. SiarScéal competitions are judged by well-respected writers, so award winners' work was my obvious starting point. The poem of my own was also included at Gwen's request.

However, largely, the choice has had to be subjective. I have selected poems that I consider to be good ones and, particularly when choosing from a number of works by the same writer, ones with an appealing subject. This subject might be one that I think will interest the varied range of potential readers of the anthology. The poem about old Irish measurements is an example of this. Sometimes though, the subject will be one that has a particular attraction for me. Hence, you will find a poem about Charlestown, 'my nearest town', and one about motherhood and school runs – subjects to be found in some of my own poems.

Have I succeeded in my selection aims? The proof of the pudding is in eating, they say but, perhaps that should be, the proof of the book is in the reading! In other words, read this anthology and see what you think. I hope you will enjoy your reading as much as I have enjoyed the editing.

I would like to thank Gwen McNamara Bond for asking me to undertake the role of anthology editor. I would also wish to offer heartfelt thanks to Gwen and the SiarScéal Festival team and to Roscommon County Council Library Services for their dedication and hard work in ensuring the continuation of the annual SiarScéal Festival. My thanks also go to Oscar Duggan of The Manuscript Publisher for his production of this anthology

Anni Wilton-Jones

Editor

Contents

A Selection from SiarScéal 2018 and 2019 – Children and Young People   123

Reflections on Climate Change

For this section on climate change, poems were commissioned from three schools – Castleplunkett National School, Castlerea; St Catherine's Senior School, Cabra in Dublin and St Josephs National School, Aughavas – from Write-On Writers' Group and from guest poet, Faye Boland. Faye has provided the following introduction to her two poems.

In 2017, I was thrilled to win the Hanna Greally International Literary Award 2017 and be awarded a publishing deal with The Manuscript Publisher.

The following year, I returned to Roscommon to attend The Beneath Western Skies Regional Art Competition and to launch my debut poetry collection, *Peripheral*. I had the pleasure of delivering a poetry workshop on *Poetry and the Senses* at the SiarScéal Festival 2018 and, after winning the Robert Leslie Boland Prize 2018 and being highly commended for the Desmond O'Grady Poetry Prize in 2019, I was honoured to be asked to judge The Hanna Greally International Adult Poetry and Short Story Competitions in 2019.

Winning the Hanna Greally Prize has been invaluable in launching my career as a Poet and Creative Writing Tutor with Kerry Education and Training Board, as it has also been to many others before me.

Faye Boland

Aftermath

by Faye Boland

Forked branches stab
the chilly air. I sit on cold
stone, watch children clamber
on rocks, unsettling the stillness
as their seagull-shrieks rise
in an airborne swirl.

Here Darwin bellowed,
uprooted stalwart oaks,
flung interwoven debris,
plastic, seaweed
at the road's edge.
This freak-tide ribbon,
vestige of the flood's threat
before it scuttled away,
sucking the wind seaward.

Burnout

by Faye Boland

after Michael Symmons Roberts

Inaudible at first —
a hairline fracture,
stretched to breaking,
a skin punctured

by parched earth,
heat rising,
air thick
with noxious gases.

Press your ear to the ground,
hear the scream
of ice-caps cracking.
A slaughter of trees,

groaning as they fall
and corkscrew winds howling —
twisting and howling —
as water rises and

we spin,
hotter and faster,
burning ourselves out.

Untitled

by Anne Murray

C. Clean cotton clouds covering

L. Lilting, lush, leafy, landscape

I. Interspersed with

M. Meandering streams.

A. Abundant

T. Trees shelter

E. Earth.

C. Charred, chopped, chaffed

H. Habitat harvested.

A. Angry avarice alters

N. Nature and navigates

G. Gouged gaping gaps in ground.

E. Evolving ecology, Earth endures.

Going Green

by Elizabeth Hannon

A recent report declared, "Insect populations on the planet decimated. Many exterminated. Without bugs on the food chain, other lifeforms will follow."

I'm helping my grandchildren to build a Bug Hotel. Imagine! After years of DDT, fly paper and swatters, I am now going to invite the buggers to be squatters.

I had a conversation with the sky

by Judith Davitt Geoghegan

Last night, I conversed with Sky.
Sky, I thought you'd die.
Me too, said Sky with a smile.
My lungs were black,
My clothes were grey –
I really had begun to decay.

My eyes were blurred thick with smog.
I couldn't see the mountain tops,

Just a never-ending fog
And a heart beating throb.
But due to a crisis
Caused by a virus
Sent to chastise,
Or even erase us,

I can now see mountains once shrouded in haze
And satellites show air cleaner these days.

While covid-19 tore the world,
Illuminating greenhouse gas,
Global warming mass,
Creaking health states,
Social malaise,
Ironically, temporarily cleared my haze.

People staying home, driving less,
Taking fewer flights and cruises,

Pollution in my air reducing,
Clothing bright, cleaner
But yet, not cooler.
If exposed to covid-19
And your air is putrefying,
It's fuel on a fire affair

The temporary experience of cleaner air.
How was your sky during the pandemic?

Poster by Castleplunkett National School students

Untitled
by Aidan Cribbin

Earth is the best stop.
Give mother nature a rest.
Win the race, keep mother nature from distress.
Fossil fuels are polluting our air.
Just stop and be aware.

– Castleplunkett National School

Poem
by Ruth Moylan

Don't be a meanie,
Recycle today
If you do

Pollution is at bay.
If you go green
You'll save the earth.
You have to now
To save the world.

I don't like people who kill the bees.
I don't like people who cut the trees.
It really makes me sad
And it's really bad
So, save our earth now.

– Castleplunkett National School

Untitled

by Ciara Fannon

Watch the earth and land.
Look at the atmosphere expand.
Some animals are becoming extinct.
They are all so horribly linked.
It makes the earth cry out with pain.
It is all so hard to explain.

– Castleplunkett National School

Think

by Michael Neary

If you kill the bees
you'll fall to your knees.
If you use fossil fuels
you are doing the environment cruel.

The earth is dying,
everything is crying
and the people are lying
while the chips are frying.

– Castleplunkett National School

Untitled
by David Nally

We need to change our way of life
Today, not tomorrow.
We need to go green
To save our bees.

We need to plant more trees to help our Earth.
We have to stop the use of pesticide.
Our earth is falling apart.
We have to act now.

Our earth is like a precious gem.
We have to mind and help it.
It's our only home; we only have one chance.
We are doing this for ourselves and each other
So, go green and save our earth now.

– Castleplunkett National School

Climate Change
by Max Noone

Global warming is hard to explain.
The earth is polluting from the sky, causing a serious
  problem to you and me.
Mother Nature can't do this by herself so come on,
  let's give her a hand.
It's drying up our beloved earth and causing pain.
Let's stop this, let's give Mother nature a rest.
We must keep the earth as clean as can be.

– Castleplunkett National School

Untitled
by Joseph McDonagh

This is our Earth,
It's a valuable place,
Better help quick,
Or it will erase.

Please plant more trees,
Oh please, oh please.
Please, stop using plastic,
Or bottles you can squeeze.

Stop leaving bottles of suntan and lotion,
Unless you want to pollute the ocean.
Butterflies are flying,
Bees are dying.

Please Help Our Earth

– Castleplunkett National School

Poster by Castleplunkett National School students

Climate Change and Me

by Abigail Birkby

Climate Change is happening right now.
We need to make some changes and I think I know
  how.
Let's recycle more and not put everything in the black
  bin.
This does not help!
It is a Climate Change sin.
The world is getting hotter and the ice will all melt.
This scares me
So we need to open our eyes and see.
But we can do this;
There is still time.
We can make the earth happy once more.
But we have to start doing the right thing and from now
  on and forever more.

– St Catherine's Senior School, Cabra, Dublin

Climate Change and Me
by Kate Flynn

I think about it every night – we do not get along.
All the things that it does,
I think is very wrong.

Although the humans invited it in,
One day our earth will be dark and dim.
The trees will be dead and the sun will dry,
And surely, all humans will later die.

Because of pollution, our nasty dilution
To our sea, our air,
Is beyond cruel and unfair.

When we litter plastic, the result is drastic:
We may kill millions and billions of things.

With dear life departing, it's all regarding,
Us littering, leaving our rubbish around.

Some of us stopped, you really should know,
But some of us haven't, oh no, no, no!
That is why there's a whole war to go,
Between Climate Change and Me.

– St Catherine's Senior School, Cabra, Dublin

Climate Change and Me
by Barbara Kukula

Our Earth is suffering
But what can I do?
Planting and recycling but, what does that do?
Our Earth is here burning
while icebergs are melting
and animals are paying a price for what humans are
taking.

– St Catherine's Senior School, Cabra, Dublin

Climate Change and Me
by Katelyn Fleming

Climate change is important.
Learn what's right and wrong for the world.
I think we can do it together.
Maybe one day, this will all be over
and then, we learned to be more of a lover.

Thanks to the teachers who taught us this.
Every day, we want to be part of this.
Change is what we want.
Help us get there; we can't do it alone
And of course, we'll work together.
No one knows what we can get through.
Gas doesn't help the earth one bit.
Everyone can make a difference if we can all commit!

– St Catherine's Senior School, Cabra, Dublin

Climate Change and Me

by Katelyn Fleming

Climate change is something that we should all be
worried about.
People protest every day about it and we have to take
matters into our own hands!
When you're on a walk, pick up litter; you can change
the world!
No bin around you? Save it for when you get home;
you can change the world!

Is it a nice summer day outside? You can walk to
school; you can change the world!
At night time, plug out all appliances; you can change
the world!
At a café they ran out of cups, bring your own
recyclable cup! You can change the world!
Each little step we take gets us closer to preventing
climate change!
We need to work together on this!
Stand strong for what we do to help, save the world!

Even the little four-year olds can save the world
because they learn from what they see.
We need to set an example for the younger people
because they will teach everyone around them!
We all know Greta, an inspiration to speak up for
what's right; we can change the world together!
Greta inspires many of us but we need to become

Greta by speaking up and doing the right thing, by
saving our futures!
I'll say it once more 'We Can Change the World
Together!'

– St Catherine's Senior School, Cabra, Dublin

Climate Change and Me

by Sarah Wray

Climate Change is……
Bad,
Not good,
The worst
But, if you can make a change
In the way you use stuff,
it will help.

– St Catherine's Senior School, Cabra, Dublin

Climate Change and Me

by Milly Pidgeon

Climate change is not alright;
We need to stop before we die.
Even though it's really hard,
It's certainly worth a try!
We can do this together!

– St Catherine's Senior School, Cabra, Dublin

Climate Change and Me!

by Claire Cooke

'Climate change is a reality.'
Pollution, pollution, pollution.
Wet area's wetter, dry areas drier.
A warmer wetter world
But what can we do?
Buy better bulbs,
Less packaging
And try not to waste the food.
We can stop climate change forever
If we all do our bit.
We could make a safer world!!

– St Joseph's National School, Aughavas, 4th Class

Climate Change and Me
by Darragh McBrien

The birds are singing in the trees and that is partly
   down to me,
I separate my rubbish into different bins: all plastic, all
   cardboard and even the tins.
If we all do the same, there will be great gain and no
   more wildlife will die in vain.
Having a cold shower when weather is hot: it saves on
   electricity; that will help a lot.
If we all do our bit and make Ireland proud, when we
   look to the sky there won't be a cloud.
So If we recycle waste, it will clean up our seas,
   protect our lovely planet, our birds and our bees.

– St Joseph's National School, Aughavas, 4th Class

Climate Change
by Millie Kennington

The ice is melting; polar bears are fretting.
The sea animals are not surviving and there's no way
of denying.
Plastic, plastic everywhere. Everyone is just throwing it
anywhere.
Why can't we all just recycle and do some more
cycles?
The air is getting warmer.
Winter days are shorter.
Everyone uses plastic but, it isn't really that fantastic
So, try and use it less
Then, that will be the start of our progress.
It is also gas and oil burning.
This is all very concerning
But don't forget, this is not just your job, it is everyone
else's too.

– St Joseph's National School, Aughavas, 4th Class

Climate Change

by Cara Mc Hugh

Climate change is happening in our world right now. It is caused by greenhouse gases.

Greenhouse gases are caused by us burning fossil fuels, driving our cars and not recycling our waste. This causes the earth to heat up and melt the Icebergs and so, our oceans rise and the people living on the coast get flooded. Climate change also causes drought in hot countries. Crops fail and people starve.

Since the coronavirus started, the earth has begun to heal itself, as people are not driving cars or flying in planes and factories are closed and not burning fossil fuels.

– St Joseph's National School, Aughavas, 3rd Class

Climate Change Story

by Glenn Mitchell

Once upon a time there was a kid called James and he lived in the countryside. It was very sunny; the skies were blue and the sun shone through the clouds. It was a perfect day for a walk. He saw the birds making nests in the trees and chirping happily. The leaves on the trees were very colourful. As James went on his walk, he passed the lake and he saw two beautiful swans floating on the top of the water. He decided to sit down and rest on the green grass beside the lake. James spotted a rabbit coming out of a hole in the ground and he saw a hedgehog coming out of the hedge. James took off his clothes and went in for a swim in the lake in his swim shorts. The water was lovely and warm. He found it very relaxing. James went home after getting all the fresh air and had a lovely warm bath and a hot chocolate to snuggle up by the fire.

– St Joseph's National School, Aughavas, 3rd Class

Climate Change

by Niall Flynn

What is climate change? Climate change is how the earth is heating up and changing.

The main reason for this is humanity. We burn coal, wood, turf and plastics. We invented the engine which releases harmful gases. We also farm cattle, which release too much methane into the air. What are the main results of climate change? The ice is melting because of the warm air! The water from the ice is joining the ocean and warming it up. This is changing our weather patterns, causing more tropical storms. With more storms, it means crops can't grow, bugs can't eat. If bugs can't eat, little animals can't eat and if little animals can't eat, then big animals can't eat. In the long run, if animals can't eat, we won't be able too.

– St Joseph's National School, Aughavas, 3rd Class

Global Warming
by Shéa Flynn

This poem is about humans causing
The air to be warming
From our fires burning.

Our harmful gases rise,
Messing with our ice.
Our oceans will arise
From all that melting ice.

These oceans will get warm,
Causing bitter storms.
Floods will be born,
Treating crops with scorn.

If crops cannot grow,
Animals stay below,
Stopping babies grow,
So they will die alone.

– St Joseph's National School, Aughavas, 4th Class

Climate Change
by Meadhbh McNamara

We can stop climate change
If we work together.
We, as a planet,
Can make life on earth better.

Here's what to do:
Stop burning fossil fuels,
Stop cutting down trees
And acting like fools.

Instead of driving, try walking or cycling –
This is one way to save the day.
We, together, can help stop climate change.
We all have a part to play.

– St Joseph's National School, Aughavas, 5th Class

Climate Change and Me

by Caoimhe Casey

Climate Change is serious.
The polar bears are sad.
The ice caps are melting,
Which is very, very bad.

The World is not what it used to be,
It's a disaster everywhere
And burning fossil fuels
Is putting pollution in the air.

There's solar panels and electric cars,
Which is making a bit of a change
But, they can't do it on their own
And it's not one bit strange.

Now we know what's happening
All around the world
And next time when you get some fuel,
Think of what you've learned

The End!!!

– St Joseph's National School, Aughavas, 5th Class

Climate Change and Me

by Matthew Canning

When changes in the earth's climate system result in new weather patterns and remain in place for a long time, this length of time can be as short as a few decades to as long as millions of years. Things like over-population, pollution, burning fossil fuels and deforestation can trigger climate change. It is everybody's responsibility to make changes in their lives to halt climate change. I can help to make a change by recycling, to not litter and by not going on holidays by plane. I can also help by reminding my Mammy to walk or cycle to certain places instead of driving. By making small changes now, we can help to make this a better world.

– St Joseph's National School, Aughavas, 3rd Class

The Climate Change Poem
by Destiny Cowdell

I walked to school today
And guess what was looking at me?
Roses and buttercups
For me and you to see.

I walked past a farmer;
He was chasing a long-gone fox.
It was hours until he got home.

The climate is changing.
We don't know what to do.
Prepare for the climate to change.
We can't stop it now
So, be aware.

But look outside at the birds you see;
At the zoo, cheetahs. Are there
More? You will see.

How swift.
How sore.
It will not change
At all

– St Joseph's National School, Aughavas, 4th Class

A Selection from
SiarScéal 2018 and 2019
– *Adults* –

Measured

by Mary Branley

(in memory of my mother)

She spoke one day on
measures I'd never heard of,
remembered
from the far away.

A "gabháil" of oats –
What would fit in your two scooped hands.
A "mám" of hay –
what your arms could encircle.

So much lost in conversions,
punts to euro,
bushels, naggins, gills
reformed into sterile metric blocks.

The measure of her
eluded me always.
Now her dwindling mind
and waning strength
slide down my "mám",
pour through my "gabháil",
gather at my feet.

River
by Bernadette Lynch

The Suck is a secret, savage. She snakes
Like mercury through Cloonagh callows.
Shards of silver pierce the bog jagged.

She is rising tonight. The pike are high,

A true daughter of Achelous, she drips
honey in your ears; laps like the tides of Canute.
Three days of Connacht rain

Make her greedy. She will swallow
You whole, with flooded plains, Suffolk rams,
Meadow sweet, sedges,

She seeps through limestone. Townlands,
Minds, she is making us feel like Noah.
She is winning.

Her eddies lure, her pulse is lethal.
It would be so easy to become
A pillar of salt, to dissolve;

She would wrap you in her tendrils.
You would be there, always,
Under a shroud of sky,

She is rising tonight. The pikes are high.

Photograph by Bernadette Lynch

Samuel

by Maria Ní Mhurchú

A beautiful bundle of joy.
A little boy
Who travelled from afar,
From a distant star,
Bringing joy to all around him.

He had to traverse deserts
With little water,
With sand blowing into
His precious eyes.
He had to walk great distances,

An angel looking after him
On his journey.
He made it
After a hard struggle
And now, he's looking up at me
As if I were the Madonna herself!

I think he's made for greatness.
May God bless him.

Samuel

le Maria Ní Mhurchú

Mo leanbhabhín álainn,
Mo bhuachaillín beag
Samuel,
Anso i'm bhaclainn agam.

Samuel
Fáigh
Breitheamh,
Ceannaire ciallmhar.

Thaistil sé ó i bhfad i gcéin.
D'eitil sé ó réiltín spleodrach,
I dteannta Eli agus na haingil.

Bhrúigh Samuel beag ar aghaidh.
Chaith sé daichead lá is daichead oíche
Sa bhfásach
Gan bia, gan uisce,
An ghaineamh de shíor-séideadh
Isteach ina shúile geal-gháireacha

Ach thairg sé leis é.
Dhein sé an bheart.
Saolaíodh é domsa
Balcaire beag breá sásta,
Lena shúile geal-gháireach
Agus a smigín aoibhinn.

Mo ghrá thú, a Samuel.
Is liomsa tusa anois
Agus geallaim duit,
Ós comhair Eli is na haingil,
Go dtabharfad aire na dTrínóide dhuit.

Twin Speed, Double Action

by Dympna Molloy

Twin speed, double action.
Up, washed, dressed
Before you know your head
Has left the pillow.
Morning calls wait for no man.

Bathroom swamped,
Toothpaste squiggled on every tap,
Hairbrush retrieved from where last left
On the wash box. In the wash box
Amid the soils of yesterday.

Laces tied, buttoned, pleated, uniformed.
Cornflakes bowled, milked and sweetened.
Lay the toast triangular,
Buttered soft and hot.
The board is set, ready for action.

Last inspection,
Cross checked, no digital aeronautics
Flying off the handle,
Just time watched
Ticked to nine o three,
Forcing the last crumb down.

Bludgeoning to education.
Lunchboxes packed to capacity.

Off on the bumper to bumper crusade.
Mammy, mammy, mammy, mammy.
Four conversations calling for attention
In orchestrated disharmony
Defy the ears. Brain runs into explosion mode.
YES
In answer to every question,
Not knowing you've agreed to a party
Of twenty-four.

Amid blinking indicators of judgements made,
You too take your chance.
Pull in. U turn.
Drop off point achieved.

Silence, silence, deafening silence.
Take a breath.
Go home
To face the avalanche of disarray
That you've contrived,
Contemplating on that one hour
Since your unremembered awakening,
Wondering how else to fill your day.

Amen

by James Conway

God is always in a western sky:
sometimes his face is a father,
a daughter, a son, a hare running

when summer comes and the yellow
of tomorrows permeate us all, every
last one, forgotten stars. The crust

of yesterdays show their weary faces
in tandem with beauty and bird call –
those velvet notes ease us, peace us,

circle us, leave us in the outskirts
of heaven. The thrush, the blackbird,
and those unnamed who haunt the skies

revel in a western rhapsody, in a western
medley recital, in a dizzy coat all our own.

Amen.

Back Home to Sligo
by Eileen Connolly

Evening clouds gather,
streetlights paint strange shapes,
create mysterious patterns
on the slippery sidewalk.

Shadows lurch and dangers loom
as I struggle up the steps
to my grey apartment block,
fingers latched onto my key-fob.

Reaching the security
of chained and bolted doors,
my aching joints remind me
that I need to quit my job,
leave this dreary city life
and return home to Sligo.

Tonight, I'll say goodbye to all the gang.
I'll pack my gear and take a flight
back home to Shannon.

A few pints in The Blackstone with the lads,
supped in tune with *Mountain Road*
reels, on Feeney's fiddle,
the weight of time and hardship lifts.
I can still recite each line
of *Dangerous Dan McGrew*, from memory,
better than the Google generation.

The craic is my medicine here in Philadelphia
and I've nobody left now, back home.

The Cows

by Aisling Kenny

They are at the end of their wintering-in.
Monolithic, placid, they sway in watchful silence
up and down the shoreline stretch.
Black and shining as beetles, they are
older than themselves and this landscape.

Their line has outlived warlords and kings, burnings
and small evictions. Through all
they stand sentinel, flick their black-silk tails.
The moist munching of cud drifts uphill on the breeze,
a language of grass.

Photograph by Conor Doherty

The Burma Road Blues

by Michael Farry

The Burma Road was the nickname given to the
Collooney – Claremorris railway line

Since that morning goods train killed my kitten,
I've been wary of such callous monsters,
dreading their officious whistles, hissings,
their relentless bulk and outrageous wheels
hustling down the Burma Line

But in between the timetables, our days
were golden with scent of sleepers, glimpse
of wild orchids, ferns, a causeway, proud above
those dammed drains and vagabond rivers
bordering the Burma Line.

One winter's evening, I watched my father
and grandfather in oilskins wave red lamps,
warn the driver of the evening train that
the way was flooded. He slowed the beast,
nursed her down the Burma Line.

I should have stayed, took my turn, mastered
the tender care of points and signals, kept ash
and whin at bay with slash hook and bushman,
become the master of spanner and fish-bolt,
pampering the Burma Road.

But I, young, entranced by school and learning
assumed that railway lines went on forever

in each direction. I thought all I ever needed
was some carefree time and a copper coin
flattened by the Burma Line.

Now that all my branches have been closed down
I return to find it disused, gone native.
You must know where to search in the briars
to find the rotting sleepers, rusted rails,
remnants of the Burma Road.

But when I listen, they're still there, awake
for the summons in their glistening wet gear,
at cottage door or level crossing gates,
ready to fetch fresh ballast, sleepers, rails,
resurrect my Burma Road.

**Michael Farry was the Overall Winner at the Hanna Greally
International Literary Awards 2019 with this poem**

Crunching Leaves

by Eugene McGivern

When we run through fallen piles,
Piles of leaves plummeted to the ground
Do we delight in their swirling flight
And take solace from the crunching sound?

Do we live with wild decrees,
That make us glad without regret
And when we hear our favourite band
Revel in the sound through tons of sweat?

Would a thunderstorm stir passions,
That riddle down like rain
And in flashes bright of lightning
Would you repeat, repeat my name?

Would we wend down a river
That we traced from its tiny source
And shoot upon its roaring rapids
And marvel, marvel in its force?

Dare we now climb a shaly reek
And survey the wonders of its summit?
Then could we say the sounds of heaven
Have blessed the love we seek upon it?

Eugene McGivern was Highly Commended in the Hanna Greally International Literary Awards 2019 for his short story, *The Display*

Violet Villa

by John (Jack) F Fallon

Sunday afternoon in neutral Ireland.
Armies round the globe at each other's throats.
In an Irish midland town the River Brosna
Winds its lovely stream past the college grounds.

A long line of boys snakes its way
Along the quiet road that leads to Tullamore,
Like war refugees you saw in films,
Or Russian prisoners in snowbound Siberia.

On a patch of ground it stood alone,
No tree or hedge or flower to shelter it,
Painted pale blue with magic panes to match
And panelled door with knocker to invite.

It was the name that intrigued me most of all:
Violet Villa in gold letters on the wall.
Like Aladdin's Palace it captivated me.
It remained a landmark on our Sunday walk

In all the times we passed in summer or in fall,
We never saw a living being issue from its hall.
It remained a house of mystery, a *Mary Celeste*.
Had it ever been built to be lived in? I thought.

Strange it is this enchanted castle I remember
And the lonely days far from home and kin.

Violet Villa just a wayside pale blue cottage
Conjuring gracious living in Venice or the Côte d'Azur.

Beyond Galway

by Mary Guckian

Turning into a laneway,
Driving towards the sea,
White clouds kept moving
Beneath western skies.
Long, lanky stems pushed
Through sand and ironstone
Where the soil had gathered
Between each crevice and
From here, flowered and bloomed.
The sound of the ocean
Taking us away from pollution
Where two women sat on
Crumpled rocks, one knitting
The other studying postcards,
Both wearing pink cotton hats.
Walking on the beach, the cool
Water refreshed my tired feet
As I absorbed the beauty of the
West of Ireland Coastline.

Photograph by Conor Doherty

Tangled
by Martin McCabe

He stood gazing into the deep blue sea.
Then he saw her.
Dark red hair and a shimmering tail, the colour of a
   starling caught in the sunlight.
But she did not smile.
Then he saw the net, her beauty tangled in its grip.
He had to save her.
Captivated by her beauty he dived in.
His lungs burned as he wrestled with the nylon.
He resurfaced and dived again.
Blood from his fingertips dyed the sea red.
Finally, he freed her from its grasp.
But she was limp, her lips no longer an inviting red but
   blue.
He propelled her to the surface.
Gasping for air he dragged her onto the beach.
Frantic, he tried to resuscitate her.
His brother found him lying in the purple heather.
"What happened?" he asked him.
"I saved her from drowning," he replied.
His brother took him by the hand and led him home.
He warmed him by the turf fire.
For his story to be true, all that was missing was the
   sea.

Swallows Under Western Skies
by Thomas Mac Mahon

Oh the swallows have lined side by side.
On electric and PT cables they wait
And with a click of your fingers, they take flight
Swishing and swooshing as if Toscanini conducts.

Evenings are getting shorter
And the temperature has dropped.
To Africa the swallows go:
Less light, brisk days till our feathered friends return

Long pants, jumpers, sweeping and bagging leaves.
Jacko lanterns, sparks in the sky, children dressing up.
Christmas, family and giving time, all delight
And say a prayer and think of those who have passed.

Winter days, drizzly rain, fires warming homes.
Easter comes and we feast on lamb
And in May, the swallows do return.
Now it's short pants, long evenings and dawn at five
  AM

Editor's note: PT = post-tension

Hedge Setter

by Noel King

They gave you that job. You learned
to know a good sapling, how deep to plant it,
how much space to leave between its neighbour and it.

You made two runs either side of the path
to your parents' front door,
protected them with lettuce wire at first
from the playful puppies, Ella and Jake,
your uncle from town brought to be raised.

You grew as your hedges grew,
stubble, a beard came on your face.
You used your father's clippers to clip your hedges;
before Tralee Races, you took particular care to
    manicure
them as the racing traffic must pass your place.

You were seventeen the day the man in heavy boots
marched between your hedges and planted
the dream in you to join the navy.
Your mother cried. Your father talked to someone
who got you a local job, a hardware business.

You were twenty-four when you linked your youngest
    sister
in her wedding gown, the path not wide enough for
    two,

her dress picking up baby leaves of green;
the greens falling of the dress again
as you handed her into the waiting Mercedes
and the old dogs, Ella and Jake, barked after you with
  excitement.

One morning, in 1987, our world woke here
to find a coat of orange dust fallen like snow overnight;
the worried claimed it ash cloud from Chernobyl,
that we would all get cancer from inhaling it.
Scientists said it was a natural occurrence.
In any case, the next rainfall washed it off your
  hedges.

Today, you've passed away. The undertakers
  shouldered
your coffin down the path between your hedges;
the hedge tops level with their elbows.

And from Nowhere, These Old Photos

by Christopher M. James

Even the stained box
swoons to a faint when I pull it,
ditching a pinch of snuff.
Inside,
shades of light hazel, tint of yellow,
a nicotine-on-forefingers age
born as
cock-and-bull black and white.

Some are stuck together
as families were entreated to do,
most curled like years
and here, behind, some careful handwriting
leaning forward on its best foot.

For one man,
his wiry hair waving off to the side
like a strong-blown flame
of a held torch

or two sisters, hands on hips
in tree trunk dresses
bordering on drag
and plastered hair from
Some Like it Hot.

Beaches peter into mists
and jetties

of rusted paper clip marks,
swimming trunks
high tide over stomachs,
ice cream cones cram to show
what fugitive happiness is.

Here's a Studio one
with serrated edges,
a fancy script at the bottom,
a paradise island backdrop,
serious money,
serious pout.

No improvising
but still a father
unnaturally pushing a pram
or a tilted hat,
a brooding Cagney spruce
and not seeing behind
a rickety fence
giving the game away.

Some miens are too far away
to prove the lives they're hiding,
the nuclear flash strike
of negatives
is yet more blinding.

For a few moments,
this is where they stopped:
a vegetable patch,
brown tenement brick,
grass in a park,

a sand pit,
an infant, a bucket
with no bucket list.

Did they ever ask
what image they'd leave
or, just do it
to leave something?
A picture for this man
before he went to war.

The lid only half-fits back,
stiffens like a box
for forgotten things.
Here's a woman,
a mother, who looks pretty
in the right play of light.

**Christopher M. James won Best Poem at the Hanna
Greally International Literary Awards 2019 for this
composition**

The Red Sky of Nightfall
by Art Ó Súilleabháin

I returned west to the sunset,
headed home towards the hills
of salmon-pink streaked horizon
towards the unreal reds of evening.
I tried to pick out the blush of lake,
guided the boat by sheer skylight
towards the reed-lined sandy shore
into the shadows of wooded islands.
I rushed to moor by the bank,
tossed trout onto damp grass,
re-racked the rods by feeling
in the darkness of boathouse.
I moved before the blue of nightfall
triggered a tumbling in the dark purple
of a tunnelled rhododendron path home,
emerging stars promising only.

Photograph by Francis Muldoon

Plainsong
by Susan Graham

Music written
in Ogham
praises God,
voices drone,
voices waver,
voices vibrate,
commingle
this sonic gesture
from side of nave,
evokes a response
from the other
developing into
a ratio of dimensions,
a stripped back, non-rhythm
rhythm
without metrical regularity,
unrelated to heartbeat,
not inspiring toes to
tap in earth-affirming gesture,
raising one above the secular,
beyond the ground
in spiritual flotation,
weightless,
escaping gravitational pull,
invoking the soul
to soar
heavenwards.

Black Boots

by Patricia Donnellan

Like sentinels,
they stood

side by side
at the water's edge.

Black boots,
with laces open

As if the owner
Had stepped out,

left them to the mercy
of the incoming tide.

A woman's boots,
well worn,

facing the path
of the setting sun.

**This poem by Patricia Donnellan was Highly Commended
at the Hanna Greally International Literary Awards 2019**

White Hyacinth
by Ann Egan

I was hanging out the clothes,
calculated clothesline's run,
washing's width worked out,
spaces and fractions and places.
I hung towels and sheets farthest
away from a water barrel,
sides all slimed grey and green:
A mud puzzle hungry for whiteness.

Bearing all strategies in mind,
I selected, stretched and pegged.
Soon I was close to the barrel.
My attention was on the laundry,
Its preservation in cleanliness.
I watched for best places for drying,
on guard always against the barrel for
its sturdy place, surety of menace.

I stepped sideways, a white light glowed,
so soft, so muted, I thought of snow
in pummelled shapes of buds embedded
in the slope down to a stream,
when all else was melted
and early wildflowers bloom.

Then I suspended all my calculations,
stood still on this patch of the earth,

for there in all beauty, all serenity,
Close to the barrel's slimed ugliness,
in glorious bloom was a white hyacinth!

All about its small world was
a chiming of music, a cathedral of bells,
leaves spread out like an angel blessing
some lost soul wandering the loneliness.

The hyacinth stood free of the clothesline
and its burdens, tolled a song of peace,
exploding on my everyday world.

Gifts Beneath Western Skies
by Susan Flynn

I step in your damp, bare footprints
As we cross the sparkling sand,
And where the little waves roll
Close by your side, I stand.
Out somewhere seals are moaning
Their haunting, magic tune;
We interlace our fingers
And gaze at the harvest moon.

I gift to you, my dearest,
The big round yellow moon.
I gift my hand in your hand
And the seals' soft siren tune,
And Western skies' last blushes
Reflected in wet sand;
For you, small foamy wavelets,
Make music where we stand.

Let us walk hand in hand, now
To our secret, hollow dune,
Where sand sift cool and softly,
Beneath the yellow moon.
My love, I give you softness.
I hum the secret tune.
I hold you close tonight, dear,
For the dawn will break too soon.

I gift you with my kisses
The salty taste wind blows,
Warm breezes to caress you,
Fine sand between your toes.
The scent of Irish moss for you
And waving fronds of dulse.
The sound of curly wavelets
In time with our own pulse.

My finger traces lyrics,
Love songs for you in sand.
The moaning seals make melody,
Sea wind and waves our band.
The words are given on breezes,
I touch your ear with shell
And slowly we dance in circles:
We are under the sirens' spell.

Photograph by Francis Muldoon

Aging Mist

by Amy Barry

I picked up a round, grey pebble
from fragments of corals and shells,
wishing to dab my feet in another ocean.
My memories were transatlantic,
swelling like musical peaks.

And all the years
I've walked by the sea,
you painted on every pebble.

Restless brown eyes,
silvered hair grown wild,
white seaweed-ragged beard fluttering,
cruising the Andaman,
your cracked fingers like spiders
on the saxophone,
every note, pure.
Your playing is warm,
spinning our favourite song –

Memories are mist,
even on a clear day.

**This poem by Amy Barry was Highly Commended at the
Hanna Greally International Literary Awards 2019**

Atmosphere
by Wiltrud Dull

The firmament above Mount Fuji sparkles with stars.
Rumbles, rising far west vibrate in the air
as wild horses gallop across the Gobi Desert.

Come twilight, the sweet aroma of vanilla
blows across the vast Indian Ocean.
The Madagascar orchids settle Australians to sleep.

In Istanbul, a Muezzin calls for the day's last prayer,
while faintly catching the music and clapping
of circle dancers, at a wedding feast somewhere in
  Greece.

A full moon shimmers across Galway Bay.
Waves lap against the harbour wall and echo the
  flapping wings
of geese, gathering for the evening in Nova Scotia.

Herdsmen scan the horizon before the sudden
  darkness.
It will be another chilly night in the Kalahari Desert
But the rhythms of Brazil warm with a last fiery glow.

In a Mexico City slum twenty-four babies are born at
  midnight.
Their mothers pray for their future, dream for them,
barely hearing children's laughter in a Tokyo school yard.

Writer's Block Solution

by Maureen Harkin

You need a harbour which will inspire you to write
again.
A place to calm your steps and lift the miasma of your
despair!
A place where time has moved on yet, somehow stood
still.
A place in Connaught where, like Davies, you can
stand and stare!

Let us go then, you and I, along the Western Way.
A medley of sights to lift your floundering soul…
A melange of beauty, deep lakes and lofty cliffs,
A salmagundi of people in this assorted coloured bowl!

Breathe in Sligo's Wild Atlantic bosom's roar.
Strandhill's exhilarating swell will rouse the muse in
thee.
Tread softly all along Rosses Point and Streedagh.
Retrace W.B.'s giant steps at his beloved Isle of
Innisfree.

Capture Raftery's heterogeneous blend of Mayo,
As spring begins to dress in all her beauty.
Explore the Greenway, Foxford, the deserted village,
The patchwork beaches of Achill in a line of shore duty.

Visit Ballyfarnon, O'Carolan's home in Roscommon.
Learn of the hardship of our miners in Arigna long ago.

Let the views over the somnolent plains of Boyle stir
you.
Stay in Castlerea and Ballintober where Suck and
Shannon flow.

Feel renewed by Lovely Leitrim's lakes and hills.
Visit Dromahair's Abbey and Fenagh's ancient walls.
Take a languid cruise on the Shannon, which will
refresh you.
Admire Lough Allen's valley and Glencar Waterfalls.

Savour the hoof-like thundering of the waves at Salthill
prom.
Galway's assemblage of theatre, races, oysters and
the craic!
Journey with the disparate myriad ragbag of tourists
Whose last words are always "Galway, we'll be back!"

They'll be back to re-climb Mayo's Holy Reek.
To walk again Leitrim's many woodland trails on a
summer's day!
To visit once more Roscommon's Strokestown Park
House
And, to watch again the sun go down on Sligo Bay!

Sport the green and red, or maroon, or the black and
white!
Wrap yourself in the green and gold, or the primrose
and the blue.
Get swallowed by the fierceness of the county passion
Where dwarfing grandeur will call you and just sit
around you.

Let us go then, you and I, along the Western Way.
Its medley of sights will revitalise your floundering core
The beauty of the landscape will rouse the muse in
  thee
The scribe will emerge, words will flow and you will
  write once more.

**Maureen Harkin was Highly Commended at the Hanna
Greally International Literary Awards 2019 for her short
story, *Borrowed Time***

Two-Tier

by Philomena Travers

Two-tier cake stand:
Two-tier society.
Priest in the parlour,
Peasants in the kitchen.
Cook the priest's breakfast
then feed the plebs.
Poor, poor Padre,
Dining on his own.
Daren't let his spoon slip.
Keep a stiff upper lip.
Try to make small talk
Then home alone.

Now the party can begin.
Bring out stout and gin.
Talk flows easily.
Eggs fried greasily.
Drink up. Eat up.
Don't be afraid to slurp.
All friends together –
Talk about the weather,
The Dáil and the clergy,
The cattle and the sheep.
Old Johnny falls asleep,
Dribble on his chin.

Start up the fiddle.
Hey diddle diddle.

Cares soon forgotten.
Have another bottle.
Women in the corner
humming along.
Martin will sing.
Then evening draws in.
Farm chores beckon.
Each to their home.
Another station over
Until next spring.

Connacht Farmer
by Anni Wilton-Jones

i) Legacy

Reared he was on the farm
and adopted by it
for it saw no difference
from father to son

save that this one
thought he was master
a delusion
tamed from him by time

so as his father was
now he too is
year in   year out
year always…   weary.

ii) Walking the Boundaries

He is visiting his acres
white in winter sun
grass rigid   sculpted
with frost-feathering

glassed to a stillness
of false depth   the river
reflects the purity
of marble reeds above

saintly the land
in its frozen vestments
but devilish to work
he knows – he's tried and failed.

iii) Surrender

he will come no more
to these fields
his path is now away
beyond

left with no living
he is leaving to live
another look
a shoulder shrugged

and then
there is only
the future
and he departing.

Photograph by James Fraher

Drowsy Maggies

by Frank Murphy

An accordion
Dragged out somewhere,
Quex Road Sundays,
Backs to the wall
Talking of the summertime,
Going home.

And the drift to Mass,
The nod.

There were rumours
Of a start somewhere.
Casuals; observations
Of the scraps of a match.
The laments for the crossing,
The red pillar post box,
Imperial signs
Hanging off the overheads.
Approved bed and board,
Crooked Jacks,
Going home
And the fleadh.

Through an open doorway
Drowsy Maggies
Drowning out

Three Dog Night –

"Mama told me not to come."

Off Life-Support
by Gavin Bourke

Fell
into the final dream
no one ever
wakes from.

Her cousin's
husband's cousin's
husband.

Had the
social script licked,
of a time
rather
than a place.

Wife was a beauty,
four young children,
two good jobs
and two good cars
to carry them.

Inwardly tired unbeknownst
from keeping
it all-going.
Fit from the bicycle,
the blood suddenly
ceased.

The heart stopped
before breaking hearts.
Too far away to be saved
for a few days.

They flicked the switch
on Wednesday
of the same week,
in his nearest hospital.
A man no more
than forty-four.

The Form

by Kieran Cullen

A pair of whiskered nostrils
Then a pair of eyes.
No ripple on the surface.
A phantom. A disguise.

The otter ventured from her holt.
She sniffed the evening air.
An evening void of birdsong
Gave her cause for care.

Her eyes rubbering
To and fro.
Something out there?
She did not know.

Returning to her holt,
She coiled up for a while
And dreamed of elvers, frogs and trout
Heaped on the bank in piles.

Then down the high bank where the snow was deep,
She made herself a slide,
First shown to her by her mother
When she was at her side.

Her father left when she was a cub
Never to return.

She still scents for his track, to no avail
Out along the bourn.

In a short while she awakens
And decides to have a look
What was happening currently
Out upon her brook.

The bitch was in a predicament
But she had to take the chance.
Emerging cautiously through the reeds,
She took a guarded glance.

Down the bank observed a form
That looked out of place –
That form remembered from her youth
It hurt her to retrace.

That form, a bang, the smell of blood
Her mother gone from her side;
A memory engendered
And no place for to hide.

A pair of whiskered nostrils
Then a pair of eyes.
No ripple on the surface.
A phantom. A disguise.

A Team of Three
by Angela Gavigan

The last time he took down the bridles and collars
From their allotted place on the stable wall
Was in the springtime of the year,
To plough 'Gleann na Bhfaoileán',
The front field,
For oats

An April day dawning,
Two horses whinnying at the stable door
And a bright sun banishing the cold of morning.

The draught mare, 'Moll'
With 'Star', her life's mate,
Sensing the purpose of the day,
Willing for work and newly shod,
Longing both for the turning of the sod.

Piece by piece
The pair were harnessed
With gently whispered words.

Bridle and bit,
Collar and harness,
Traces, girth, coupling and reins.
The shining leather straps creaked under strong
   hands,
Tightened, bent back and clasped.

Photograph by Matthew Carey

Star's huge heart throbbed in her chest.
Brass buckles shone.

Hitched then,
The lightest flick of reins and the brown earth turned,
Smoothed and burnished by the ploughs bright blade.
Bonds such as theirs
One of a kind.
You'd think he drove them with his mind.

But they knew their task
As he did:
Their part in earth's renewal.
Seagulls trailing and flailing in their wake
For every juicy jewel.

A team of three,
Each exemplifying power, patience and grace
In varying measure, at every pace.
An acre a day.
A ten-mile walk.

Today, I took the bridles down from the stable wall,
Their stitches frayed and falling open.
Leathers cracked and hard
Distressed.
Their brass buckles
Green and rigid.

I remember the man who carefully closed each buckle
   for the last time,
Forty-eight spring-times ago.
Who revered his family,

His animals
And land

And, who holds my heart as tight
As once he held my hand.

Churning Days

by Katherine Noone

Ours is barrel shaped,
secured on a stand.
Six of us children line up
to turn the handle.

The splashing sound subsides
as cream converts to butter.
Mother salts, shapes
and stores it.

In years of food rationing,
we give thanks for this gift.

Going Back

by Anne McManus

After years of sitting on the ditch,
The city fathers made a 'ring' road
Through the town.
A barbarous act
Of demolition, relocation,
Self-important roundabouts
Hoping to get a mention on AA Roadwatch;
You could be in Rosses Point before you know it.
I never use it.

The old road takes me home direct:
Past the expanding cemetery,
Past the cenotaph,
Where a handful of Protestants
Stood furtively each year on Poppy Day.
Past the Cathedral,
Whose spire was the highest point in town
Until the cranes moved in.

Nowadays, the house has a royal blue door;
Once it was bright red.
The house where W.B. Yeats's aunt,
Mrs Robin Gorman, had lived
Opposite the cut stone building
With the tower on the roof
From where W.B.'s uncle
Spied his ships docking in the harbour.

In the hall, three horses still drink from a trough:
Polly, Belle and Ben.
Beside them, the barometer my father tapped each
    morning
Out of force of habit,
Giving us the cue to wet the breakfast tea.

The range crammed with steaming pots,
Soda bread cooling on the open window,
Lines of sheets blowing in the garden,
Three fires to be tended,
Foxford blankets, eiderdowns
On every bed – once my home.

Nowadays, rooms unused,
Living narrowed into three or four.
The struggle to keep dampness out,
Lighting the occasional fire
Hoping no crows have nested since last year.
Books, vinyl records, photos, pictures
Destined for the skip
When the time comes.

Well-tended gardens, front and back,
Bring unexpected colour to this grey street,
Standing out in the aerial photo
On last year's charity calendar.
Plants now fed by granules from a packet;
My mother's treasured roses do not seem to mind
The change from farmyard manure.

These days, no families in the street.
The neighbours come at nine and leave at five.

Gold lettered windows offer
Legal services (divorce included), chiropody,
Dental implants, oil fills, specialist coffees,
And, most recently, tattoos.

Summer Recaptured

by Gearoid O'Brien

Their idle summer mornings
Spent swimming in the river
Where it foamed over the weir
Near a hump-backed bridge.

Three passionate sisters
Riding down to the river
Bareback in night-gowns,
The air cooling their skin.

Three free spirits
Plunging in and tumbling
Over the cascade
To be washed downstream.

Three tethered horses,
Their owners delighting
In being caressed by
The dark green weeds

Swimming on, carefree,
Before being washed up
Like wreckage from the shallows
To mount their horses for home.

Photograph by Deirdre Kennedy

Galway Greys
by Eithne Cavanagh

All around is monochrome today.
I watch the undulating of the sea.
The sky creates a dome of dove soft grey.

Gulls cavort above the silver spray.
I marvel that they soar and swoop so free.
All around is monochrome today

In their skyward frolicking and play,
Perhaps the gulls are beckoning to me.
The sky creates a dome of dove soft grey.

The Aran Islands seem to float away
Like shrouded boulders in the pewter sea.
All around is monochrome today.

At Nimmo's Pier the large waves slap and flay,
A herring gull shrieks loud her wicked glee.
The sky creates a dome of dove soft grey.

If you ask me where I would like to stay,
I'd answer, "Here, where you and I can see
That all around is monochrome today
And the sky is still a dome of dove soft grey."

The Fall

by Patrick Devaney

Across the saturated hill
long, bright shafts of sunset
enter the Colleen's side
where fallen leaves have left it bare.

A woodbine, the last survivor
of all that graced the trees,
spins lightly on its stem –
a fairy dancer, all unseen.

Below, the twilit, earthen floor,
moss-grown and strewn with leaves,
tempts beauty from its bough,
to rest awhile till darkness falls.

Yielding, the flower drops lightly down,
petals soak earth's moisture
destined, with sister blooms,
to make a mulch for exposed roots.

A blackbird skims the hazel maze,
lights nimbly, then proceeds.
A woodland undertaker
to investigate the flower,

With muted note, it flutters off
Leaving, to fill the void,

the twitching of bare twigs
under a sharp, autumnal cold.

Under Atlantic Light

by Pearse Murray

Under Atlantic light,
Sea mirrors to its depth
the sky of sun, moon and
peeling the lonely stars from infinity.

The wind strokes it.
Our modest star polishes it and
our moon moves it.

Throw-back memories come surfacing
for past summer days on a sand-dunned edge
where dad skimmed flat discs of time.

With the quick of their bounce of hard
and the quick of their scrape of water,
as the quick of this ephemeral beat return.

From the collapsing waves racing
and drawing in the blue, the still and
the eyes' silent casts on light,

memory blasts all the laminations of time,
that tugs and freezes this singularity
of a bonding sponges' spacious presence.

Rinn Dúin

by Sinéad MacDevitt

I come from a place on a headland
that juts out onto Loch-Rí:
a place with a Norman castle
built in the twelfth century.

I come from a place with a market,
a hospital, church and mill.
Little remains but a fort and field
and a skeletal stony wall.

I come from a place claimed by Éire
during the thirteenth century:
a place that was sacked and garrisoned
and that's barely a memory.

A place where murmurs from the breeze
since the fourteenth century,
carries voices of forefathers
back to my birthplace by Loch-Rí.

Atlantic Footprints
by Carol Caffrey Witherow

The slipway's mossy home to the upturned boat
that squats upon the rocks. A ruffle of seaweed,
severed from its kin, waves forlornly
at the receding tide. Here, in this cove,
where the mountains dip their craggy toes into the
  ocean,
here is where you loved to swim. I still see you in slow
  motion.

Our childhood Irish sea was lava-hot compared to this.
Here, I lower myself inch by parsimonious inch
into the polar cold; you gasp, smile, submerge yourself
and cleave your way towards the headland.
"It's just like soup," you quote our dad.
I used to think you were half-dolphin. Or half-mad.

That cloudless day, attended by the sheep up in the
  bracken,
I wondered where you found the strength to dive into
  each day,
abandoning the pain behind you like a discarded towel.
I wondered if there would be more swims, more days,
  like this.
So many things beneath the surface, content to be
  unspoken;
the water bore the weight and left the silence
  unbroken.

One day, the dolphins came to this secluded place.
They paused beyond the headland and did their dance
   for you.
You watched alone, entranced, then waved to them as
   they moved on.
I'm glad you had that moment. The ripples left behind
   you,
your footprints in the water, are enduring as the seas.
Adieu, my dearest sister. Swim in peace.

Beneath Western Skies

by Eilish Dunning

Across the valleys,
Across the seas,
Across the distant miles,
There's a beauty that surrounds us
Beneath western skies.

As the sun rises on the mountain
And the moon hides behind a cloud,
There's a swarm of migrant birds
Chirping out loud.

They are seeking out a new home
In countries far and wide,
As they fly across the ocean
Beneath western skies
Take a look around you
And see the beauty of this isle.
It's been here from the beginning
And where my heritage lies.

There's no place on this earth
That I would rather spend a while,
Than sharing all my dreams with you
Beneath western skies.

Sunday in Central Park

by Bernadette Bradley

See Central Park:
An icy incandescence
Lights a fallen Eden
Whose shivering skyline
Shields a tale of towers.
Sirens silenced in a Sabbath shroud

But wait, the scene is set
And despite the die,
Amidst a shuffle of resigned extras,
Hapless homo sapiens stride and strut
And dance their denial
On their infamous frontier.

Now watch as the daydream dissolves
And despondency descends,
Pulling the day down
And the park into paralysis.
See central park:
A still in the frame of tarnished towers
And frightened skies
Under constant review.

Across the Pond
by Laura Carroll

A short hop across the pond, just beyond the horizon
As the immense blue curves with the earth
Is where you are.

Or, is the coffin ship still on route,
Its cargo dreaming of the day they set foot on dry land,

That island,
A cacophony of foreign tongues
Where you'll be re-baptised?

Remember home as she welcomes you in
With promises of freedom, a new life – live it well

And whenever you find us cross your idle mind,
Look out over the sea to where your true heart lies:
Back home, underneath these western skies.

Milk Lady of Athlone
by Bridie Breen

Bridie Galvin arrived every
Monday morning, winter or
summer, 7.30am sharp.

Bicycle balanced carefully
Then, the ring of her bell,
Three quick determined tinkles.

She lifted the lidded jug
off the handlebars.
Small pearl drop splashes
glistened in the early light.
Enamel sides decorated from within.

Headscarf knotted tight under chin,
Her stone bead eyes
encased in a granite face.
A blue hue on pursed lips
endowed her with a ferocious
expression and she would look
me up and down before asking,
in her country brogue,
"Do ya want any today?"

A quick run indoors to my mother,
sandals clicking on tiled floor.
I'd race back to say,

"Two pints of buttermilk, Mrs Galvin, please."
Her face would soften when
I exchanged a few bob.

Two empty bottles clinked,
Enwrapped by icy fingers,
Spout firmly held and not a drop spilt.
I never knew if the timidity of saying please
was gifted with a smile or, her relief
at the lighter load,
As she battled wind and rain
up the gravelled hill.
My thoughts remained transfixed
with the soda bread expected
at the end of a school day.

Poseidon Rises

by Mae Newman

The turbulent Atlantic is tranquil.
A stripped stone shines on a Clare beach.
I bend to pick it up yet, conscience niggles.
As I can resist everything except temptation,
It goes into my pocket. I thread the briny water.
The azure sky turns gunmetal grey.
Waves rise with a thunderous roar,
Arriving on the beach like a Viking invasion.
Mystical music fills the air.
Sea nymphs crawl up from the ocean bed.
My feet sink and swirl in the revolving sand;
Pebbles lash at my toes as Lords of the Wind
Get their revenge. I throw back the stone; music fades,
The turbulent Atlantic is tranquil.

Found in Ballinahinch Wood

by Ita O'Donovan

Robert Frost was on my mind today.
Unlike his silver birch,
this one is standing
tall and smooth and straight
like a young girl not yet budded,
or a boy's young body, still pliant,
unbowed by western storms.
Nearby, hugging earth,
the remains of a fallen tree
has a carapace of roughened bark,
where adhesions of stray growth
have found a home.
Further in, the pattern on the river replicates
the considered marks of a Le Brocquy tapestry.
There is an ambiguous plop in the water
and far above the wind-zither plays the leaves.
The birds are not insistent,
as if overawed by ancient time
visible in the roots twisting on the path
polished by many feet
and in the stepping stones gathered, bedded-in,
by hands in another century.
A waterfall of moss
with slow velvet fertility
seems thrown there to soften my eyes.
There's a muffled musk of leaf mould
and stilled life of the insect world:
a compost for renewal.

Meandering Beneath Western Skies

by Maureen Lydon

Suck, brimfull of fish,
Lake O'Flynn to Shannonbridge.
Fisherman's delight,

where once the corncrake,
in clover-scented meadows,
clattered all night long,

now fantastic light
looked through the eyes of bridges
spanning ancient fords,

stone walls are cushioned
with plush tussocks of green moss
divide fields nearby,

in the dense heather
the grouse wings his heavy flight
nesting place disturbed,

bleating drumming sounds,
the zig-zag flight of the snipe
over the water,

kingfisher splash dives
from a bough that arches low,
glinting flying jewel,

nocturnal creature
sulks the otter in his den.
Dark brown water dog,

Longing for the sea,
your fluid force drives you,
towards your ultimate goal.

Whistler

by Christine Broe

His hair raked by the wind,
He whistles, his back to the sea,
Bathed in orange light. He breathes,
Laments the sinking sun.

Around him, a huddle of music men
Play welcome to the night,
Perched on the edge of the world
With fiddle, squeeze box and pipes.

A singer sits on the cliff edge,
Draws notes up through his bones.
His hands feel the vibrations
As the sound escapes his throat.

When dark set, the men slink homewards,
Shadows follow them long and blue
But the whistler wraps himself
In tunes, in dreams, in wool,

Beds down in the rocks, back to the west,
His whistle close to his chest.
At first light, he'll join the chorus of bird;
Sing to waking sun and breaking day.

It is Written in the Arch of the Sky –
John Ruskin
by George Walker

Their name escapes me in the sun
my shadowed memory losing where I stored
this shape of fading lilac
sun-bleached month withered
they hang their skirts in dry surrender

beyond the pergola fuchsia bee-tremble
nod to waving birch and ash
the lake plays hide and seek
behind a lime screen

I count colours in the Professor's Garden
six tones of purple three shades of pink
two yellows and so many greens
I abandon need

through my shadows Clematis cling to the pergola
leaves breeze pattern the page of the sky
dapple the path

I smile at remembering
that recaptured name
smile for that smile

Smile for tomorrow
when I will sit in other shadows
remember this.

The Poacher

by Sinead McClure

No fisherman at night
In the quiet of this glen
Would tease the thin cloth
Of calm on this river's back
With a slash hook
Slicing against the current.

Struggling with the knapsack,
Straps dig into your shoulders
As you power up the spotlight, drench our view.

Standing as a wayward alder sapling,
Watery roots purchased,
You waver, then thrash.

A splash cuts the water clean, one sweet movement
That sends the catch neatly to rest at our feet.

We bag the flapping prize
The light quenched.
Our eyes adjust, we move on.
Wet roots slosh behind us.

A Selection from
SiarScéal 2018 and 2019
– Children and Young People –

Spray Colours

by Chloe Fleming

The sea splashes through the water
Like little raindrops
Twinkling around the whirling sky.
In the splash of the wave,
are the colours of a rainbow.
Now for me,
waves will never be the same
As they are today.

– Dromahair Library

Haiku

by Joshua Lawn

I feel sad for bees.
They sorrowfully sting their predator,
With no hope of living.

– Dromahair Library

Photograph by Anni Wilton-Jones

Pawprint and Patch

by Fiadh Keogh

"I want out of the garage," said Pawprint.

"We should be let out soon," said Patch. "Wait, I think I hear something, Pawprint."

Patch called up to Pawprint, who was up on the second to top surfboard. Then, the garage door opened. Patch ran out with Pawprint close behind her.

"I am going to go into the trees over there," Patch said.

"Me, too," Pawprint replied. He ran into the trees with Patch.

"Oh look, there's Buster," said Patch, "I want to run around the house. Hey Buster, you can't catch me!"

They ran around the house five times, then Pawprint ran into the pillar and Patch ran up a tree.

Then, the owners called Buster in and fed the kittens, then went to bed. Pawprint purring around Patch said, "Yes Patch, I want to do the same thing again tomorrow" … and they did.

– Dromahair Library

The Cat

by Caoimhe Maguire

From a little bundle of fun,
to a majestic creature
with a loud meow
and a gentle purr.

From a tiny kitten,
small and frail,
to a large, graceful creature
with thin, delicate stripes
from head to tail.

From a small creature,
squeaky and loud,
to a strong cat,
quiet and proud
that makes no sound
as it walks around
on padded feet.

From a playful kitten
that runs and bounds
all over the place,
to a creature that
walks with liquid grace.

– Aughavas National School

Lighthouse
by Grace McIntyre

The smooth diamond
shining in the sea;
what fun I could have
in the sun.
My Lighthouse stands,
waiting to save
a life or maybe two.
It could be you.
How much you would
be grateful for
a life-saving lighthouse.

– Aughavas National School

Man and Dog Paddle in the Sea

by Kate McCarthy

Walking through the water,
it's cold, refreshes my mind,
filled with memories
collected over time.

We've been through many hardships.
We left them all behind.
Forever, I will stick with him,
until the end of time.

Walking towards the horizon,
I see a brand-new start.
I am his loyal pet,
so we will never part.

We are two best friends
That were destined to verge
But the sight to others
is simply man and dog.

– Bunnanaddan National School

Feeding the Birds

by Amy McCarthy

The girl by the shore,
she walks alone
But years ago,
she was more at home.

As the sun leans down,
her feet brush the sand,
As the tide creeps by,
wondering why the old days
used to fly.

Walking along the shore,
everything comes back
for one moment more:
From beak to bread
and bread to beak,
closer and closer
to her peak.

The sand dunes
come undone.
Birds fly away
one by one.
Figure left forgotten;
one can't take no more.
Her shadow leaves the sand.
The beach is plain and bland.

– Bunnanaddan National School

Fiery Sunset
by Sara Nally

Red hot, fiery flames
burst out in the sky.
It doesn't burn a branch
or twig but it does burn
your eyes with its
bright red, dark orange and
darkened cloud.
It will give us a beautiful
day tomorrow.
Summer is my time.
Beautiful golden sunshine
during the day;
gorgeous, red, fiery sunsets
at night. I never want it to end.

– Castleplunkett National School

Photograph by Anni Wilton-Jones

Under Western Skies

by Ian Kearney

On our farm,
We have our highs and lows.
In the barn, the cows lie low.
Mark Cribbin spreads the slurry.
John pulls the bull out of the pond.
The Fiat 110 90 mowing, mowing.
In summer, that's the way we go.

– Castleplunkett National School

Under Western Skies

by Joshua Hussey

The seas are blue.
Our environment will not do.
Global warming is such a matter.
Our county is such a splatter.
The country is still green
But in towns, it is not clean.
The wind is blowing
Now the rain is showing.
We are cutting fields
But not stopping at yields.
People eating junk food
And then going into a mood.
The roads are narrow;
You should see people
With their tractor and harrow.
The cows are mooing
While we are chewing,
Not blinking, not even thinking
About how lucky we are.
Under the western skies.

– Castleplunkett National School

Grace Waldron, Castleplunket National School

Charlestown, Co. Mayo
by Aine Keenan and Zara Hunt

Edged on the town's verge
Where pavements burst in colourful bloom,
Plants on pavements,
The elegant, ebony sculpture
Poses in dance.
Cars move swiftly by.
Memories from Roscommon Town,
Similarities of place,
Brought me to the musical figurines.
In harmony with life itself,
Dancing in circled
Musical rhythm,
Unity in time.
Traditional, attracting tourists
To the joy, fun and warmness of music and dance

– Convent of Mercy, Roscommon

A Cold Winter's Night

by Thays Alves Ferreira

She walked down the street
On a cold winter's night.
The events of this day
Flashing in her mind.
She stops on the bridge
And smiles as she sees
The light shine on the river.
Her grin faded as she thinks,
Who will miss me when I die?

– Convent of Mercy, Roscommon

Mark Lee, Castleplunket National School

Wonders of Spring
by Luke Keane

Once again, out of the darkness
A new light flickers.
Animals who have persevered,
Endured the endless winter.

A new wind brings a new age,
An age of life.
The birds with rested voices sing anew.
Flowers arise from their endless sleep.

Everything unifies to create the marvels
And wonders of spring.

– Roscommon Community College

Colours of the Sky
by Seán Egan

I gaze up in wonder as
The sky shifts in colour,
From blue to red to
Pink until it all climaxes
In an explosion of colour.
Until it dies out and lets
The neutral black envelops
The sky. Yet, as quickly as
It escaped, the colour
Returns in the form of
Endless quasars.
I then frown, knowing these
Colours died long ago
But I find solace and appreciation
For them, as they have travelled
Light years just to perform an
Extravaganza of beautiful
Colour for our night sky.

– Roscommon Community College

Acknowledgements

Patronage

Roscommon County Council Library Services for offering SiarScéal a home since 2007, for your patronage and sponsorship throughout the years especially to County Librarian, Sandra Turner, Mary Butler, Meliosa McIntyre and all the library staff for your ongoing support and Council funding.

In Association with:

Roscommon, Ballinamore and Tubbercurrry Libraries for hosting the Beneath Western Skies exhibition and workshops. Participating schools, secondary and ongoing, namely Castleplunkett, Aughavas, Bunnanaddan National Schools, the Dromahair Library book club children and St Catherine's Senior School, Cabra, Dublin. Also, the principals and teachers for embracing SiarScéal. Local writers, national and international who annually write for the Hanna Greally International Literary Awards competition. Poet Faye Boland. Oscar Duggan of The Manuscript Publisher. Sligo photographers who provided many of the illustrations for this anthology.

SiarScéal's *Beneath Western Skies* anthology is produced in association with SiarScéal committee member, author and photographer, Anni-Wilton Jones, who compiled and edited this anthology.

Sponsors

**Comhairle Contae
Ros Comáin**
Roscommon
County Council

Clár Éire Ildánach
*Creative Ireland
Programme*
2017—2022

SiarScéal is supported by the Creative Ireland Programme,
an all-of-Government five-year initiative, from 2017 to 2022,
which places creativity at the centre of public policy. Further
information from www.creative.ireland.ie and www.ireland.ie